Forms at Your Fingertips

Table of Contents

D1611794

About This Book

Inside this all-new compilation—*Forms at Your Fingertips*—you'll find hundreds of handy forms to help you manage your classroom, plan instruction, and communicate with both students and parents. Designed in seasonal and open formats, you'll find forms such as lists and labels, notes and organizers, and posters and planning sheets that you can use time and time again throughout the entire year! *Forms at Your Fingertips* is one resource you can't be without!

Managing Editor: Cindy Daoust
Editor at Large: Diane Badden
Copy Editors: Tazmen Carlisle, Amy Kirtley-Hill, Karen L. Mayworth, Kristy Parton, Debbie Shoffner, Cathy Edwards Simrell
Art Coordinators: Theresa Lewis Goode, Stuart Smith
Artists: Pam Crane, Theresa Lewis Goode, Clevell Harris, Ivy L. Koonce, Clint Moore, Greg D. Rieves, Rebecca Saunders, Barry Slate, Stuart Smith, Donna K. Teal
The Mailbox® Books.com: Judy P. Wyndham (MANAGER); Jennifer Tipton Bennett (DESIGNER/ ARTIST); Karen White (INTERNET COORDINATOR); Paul Fleetwood, Xiaoyun Wu (SYSTEMS)

President, The Mailbox Book Company™: Joseph C. Bucci
Director of Book Planning and Development: Chris Poindexter
Curriculum Director: Karen P. Shelton
Book Development Managers: Cayce Guiliano, Elizabeth H. Lindsay, Thad McLaurin
Editorial Planning: Kimberley Bruck (MANAGER); Debra Liverman, Sharon Murphy, Susan Walker (TEAM LEADERS)
Editorial and Freelance Management: Karen A. Brudnak; Sarah Hamblet, Hope Rodgers (EDITORIAL ASSISTANTS)
Editorial Production: Lisa K. Pitts (TRAFFIC MANAGER); Lynette Dickerson (TYPE SYSTEMS); Mark Rainey (TYPESETTER)
Librarian: Dorothy C. McKinney

www.themailbox.com

Classroom Management

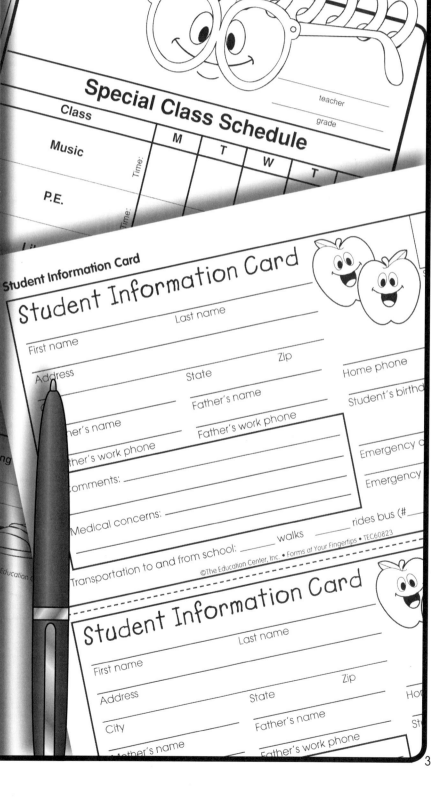

Behavior Documentation

	Date	Action Taken	Parent Contact/R...

Special Class Schedule

teacher _____

grade _____

Class		M	T	W	T
Music	Time:				
P.E.	Time:				

Student Information Card

Student Information Card

First name _____ Last name _____

Address _____ State _____ Zip _____ Home phone _____

...her's name _____ Father's name _____ Student's birthd...

...her's work phone _____ Father's work phone _____ Emergency ...

...comments: _____ Emergency ...

Medical concerns: _____ rides bus (# _____

Transportation to and from school: _____ walks _____

©The Education Center, Inc. • Forms at Your Fingertips • TEC60823

Student Information Card

First name _____ Last name _____

Address _____ State _____ Zip _____ Ho...

City _____ Father's name _____ St...

Mother's name _____ Father's work phone _____

August

©The Education Center, Inc. • Forms at Your Fingertips • TEC60823

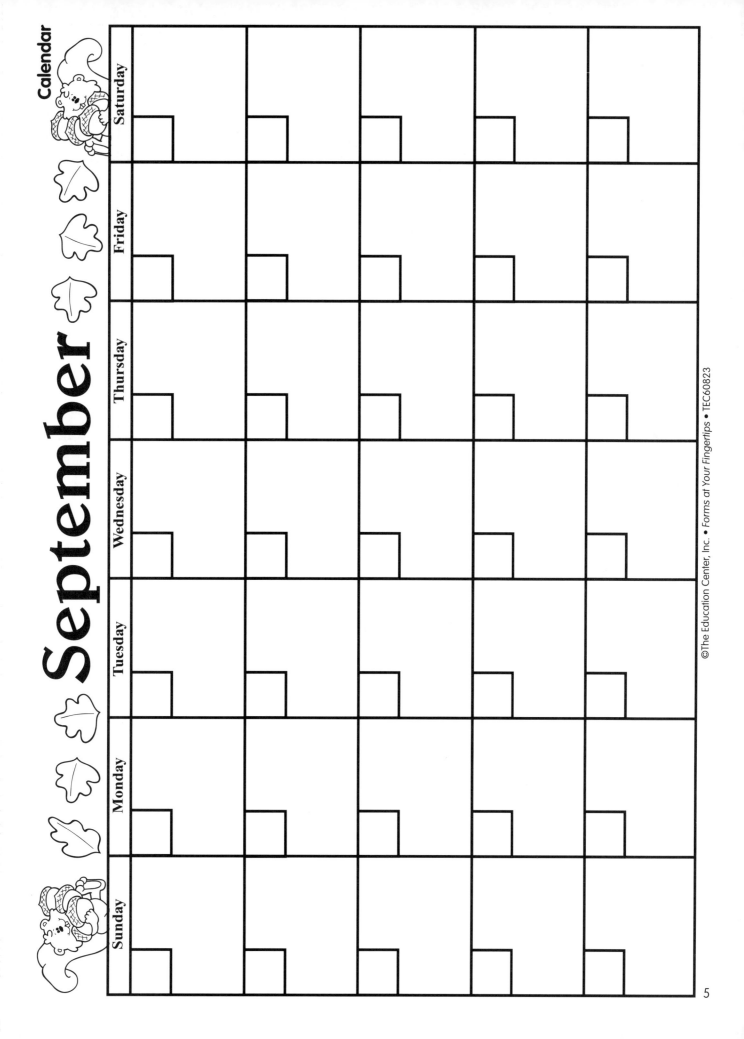

Calendar

September

Sunday	Monday	Tuesday	Wednesday	Thursday	Friday	Saturday

©The Education Center, Inc. • Forms at Your Fingertips • TEC60823

5

Calendar

OCTOBER

Sunday	Monday	Tuesday	Wednesday	Thursday	Friday	Saturday

6

©The Education Center, Inc. • Forms at Your Fingertips • TEC60823

November

Sunday	Monday	Tuesday	Wednesday	Thursday	Friday	Saturday

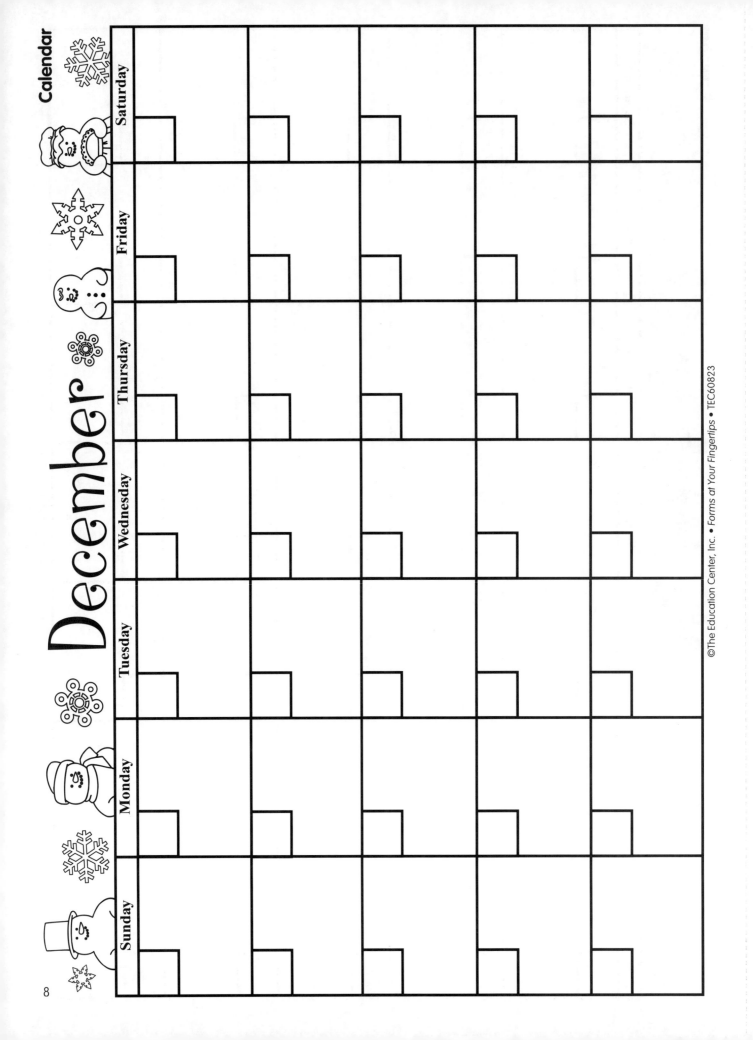

Calendar

December

Sunday	Monday	Tuesday	Wednesday	Thursday	Friday	Saturday

January

Sunday	Monday	Tuesday	Wednesday	Thursday	Friday	Saturday

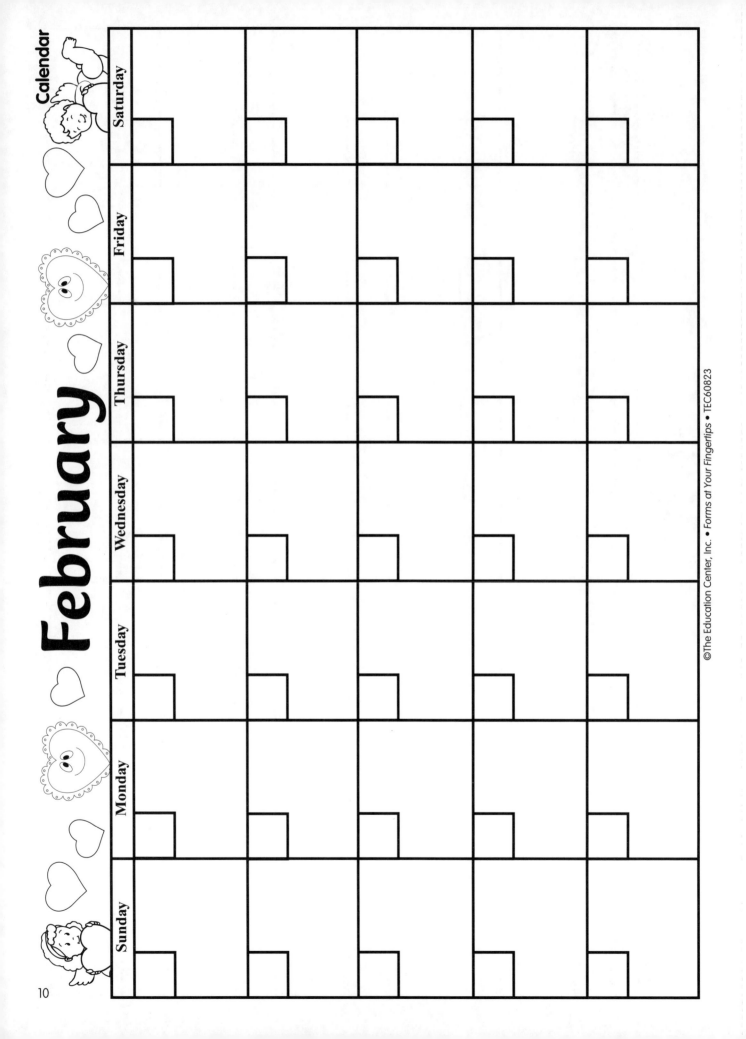

February

Calendar

Sunday	Monday	Tuesday	Wednesday	Thursday	Friday	Saturday

10

March

Sunday	Monday	Tuesday	Wednesday	Thursday	Friday	Saturday

April

Sunday	Monday	Tuesday	Wednesday	Thursday	Friday	Saturday

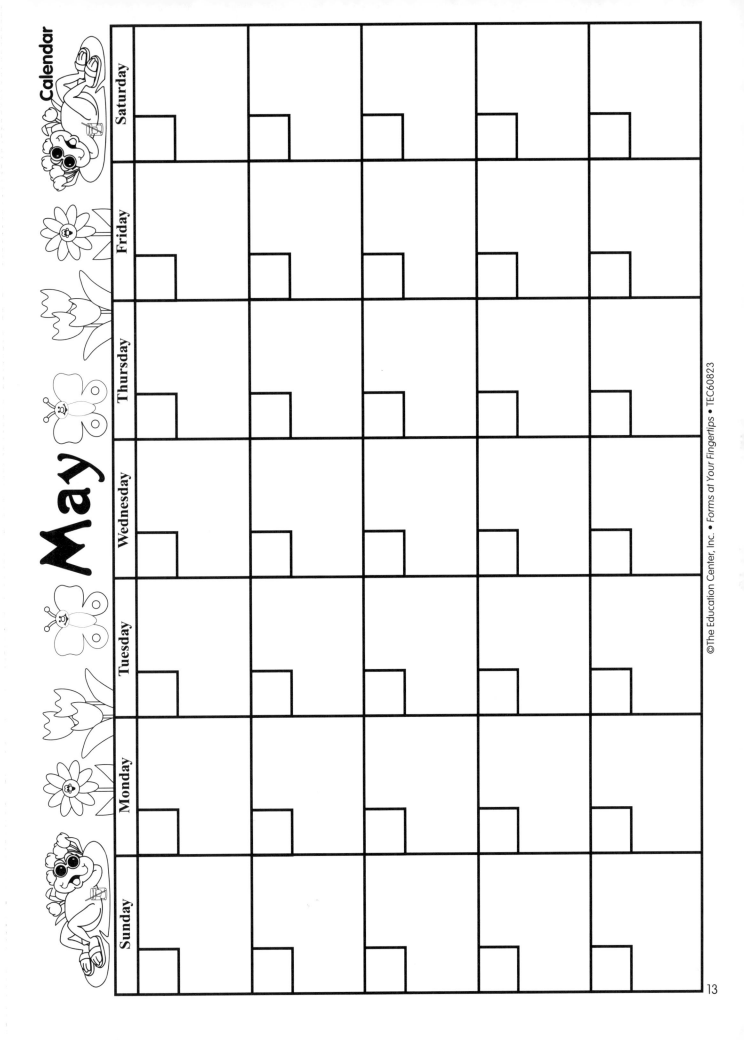

Calendar

May

Sunday	Monday	Tuesday	Wednesday	Thursday	Friday	Saturday

Calendar

June

Sunday | Monday | Tuesday | Wednesday | Thursday | Friday | Saturday

July

Sunday	Monday	Tuesday	Wednesday	Thursday	Friday	Saturday

Student Information Card

First name   Last name

Student no.

Address

City   State   Zip

Mother's name   Father's name   Home phone

Mother's work phone   Father's work phone   Student's birthdate

Comments: _____

Medical concerns: _____

Emergency contact:

Emergency phone:

Transportation to and from school: _____ walks _____ rides bus (#____) _____ other

©The Education Center, Inc. • *Forms at Your Fingertips* • TEC60823

Student Information Card

First name   Last name

Student no.

Address

City   State   Zip

Mother's name   Father's name   Home phone

Mother's work phone   Father's work phone   Student's birthdate

Comments: _____

Medical concerns: _____

Emergency contact:

Emergency phone:

Transportation to and from school: _____ walks _____ rides bus (#____) _____ other

©The Education Center, Inc. • *Forms at Your Fingertips* • TEC60823

Class Information

	Name	Birthday	Parent Name	Home No.	Work No.
1.					
2.					
3.					
4.					
5.					
6.					
7.					
8.					
9.					
10.					
11.					
12.					
13.					
14.					
15.					
16.					
17.					
18.					
19.					
20.					
21.					
22.					
23.					
24.					
25.					
26.					
27.					
28.					
29.					
30.					

Transportation List

Teacher: _____

Room No.: _____

Grade: _____

Walkers

Bus Riders

Bus #

Car Riders

Other

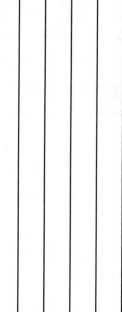

©The Education Center, Inc. • Forms at Your Fingertips • TEC60823

Student Lunch and Snack List	Daily Lunch					Weekly Lunch or Milk	Milk or Ice Cream				
	M	T	W	Th	F		M	T	W	Th	F
1.											
2.											
3.											
4.											
5.											
6.											
7.											
8.											
9.											
10.											
11.											
12.											
13.											
14.											
15.											
16.											
17.											
18.											
19.											
20.											
21.											
22.											
23.											
24.											
25.											
26.											
27.											
28.											
29.											
30.											

Class List: Back-to-School

	1.													
	2.													
	3.													
	4.													
	5.													
	6.													
	7.													
	8.													
	9.													
	10.													
	11.													
	12.													
	13.													
	14.													
	15.													
	16.													
	17.													
	18.													
	19.													
	20.													
	21.													
	22.													
	23.													
	24.													
	25.													
	26.													
	27.													
	28.													
	29.													
	30.													

1.											
2.											
3.											
4.											
5.											
6.											
7.											
8.											
9.											
10.											
11.											
12.											
13.											
14.											
15.											
16.											
17.											
18.											
19.											
20.											
21.											
22.											
23.											
24.											
25.											
26.											
27.											
28.											
29.											
30.											

Class List: Winter

1.												
2.												
3.												
4.												
5.												
6.												
7.												
8.												
9.												
10.												
11.												
12.												
13.												
14.												
15.												
16.												
17.												
18.												
19.												
20.												
21.												
22.												
23.												
24.												
25.												
26.												
27.												
28.												
29.												
30.												

1.														
2.														
3.														
4.														
5.														
6.														
7.														
8.														
9.														
10.														
11.														
12.														
13.														
14.														
15.														
16.														
17.														
18.														
19.														
20.														
21.														
22.														
23.														
24.														
25.														
26.														
27.														
28.														
29.														
30.														

Class List: Summer

	1.														
	2.														
	3.														
	4.														
	5.														
	6.														
	7.														
	8.														
	9.														
	10.														
	11.														
	12.														
	13.														
	14.														
	15.														
	16.														
	17.														
	18.														
	19.														
	20.														
	21.														
	22.														
	23.														
	24.														
	25.														
	26.														
	27.														
	28.														
	29.														
	30.														

WEEKLY ACTIVITY SCHEDULE

Time	Monday	Tuesday	Wednesday	Thursday	Friday

teacher

grade

Special Class Schedule

Class		M	T	W	T	F
Music	Time:					
P.E.	Time:					
Library	Time:					
Art	Time:					
Computer	Time:					
	Time:					

Students attending other classes: _____

_____

_____

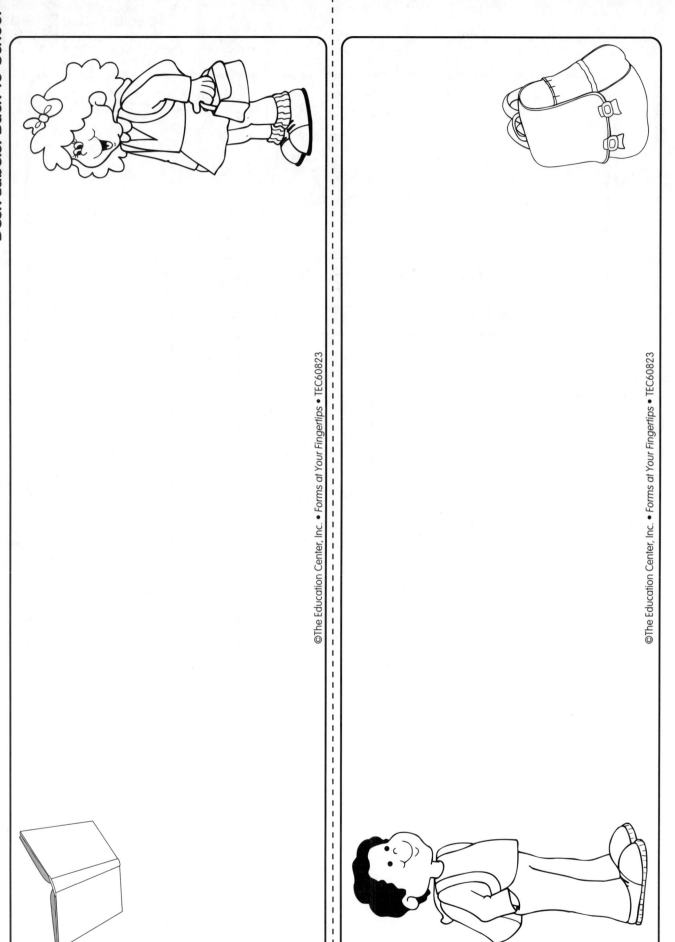

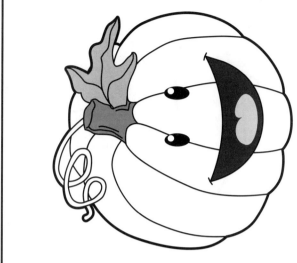

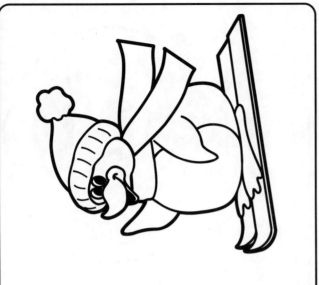

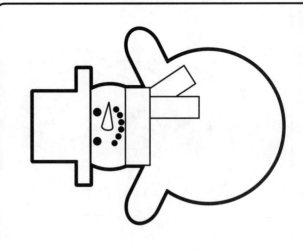

LEARNING CENTER STARS

Name	Math	Reading	Art	Blocks	Manipulatives	Writing	Dramatic-Play	Discovery		
1.										
2.										
3.										
4.										
5.										
6.										
7.										
8.										
9.										
10.										
11.										
12.										
13.										
14.										
15.										
16.										
17.										
18.										
19.										
20.										
21.										
22.										
23.										
24.										
25.										
26.										
27.										
28.										
29.										
30.										

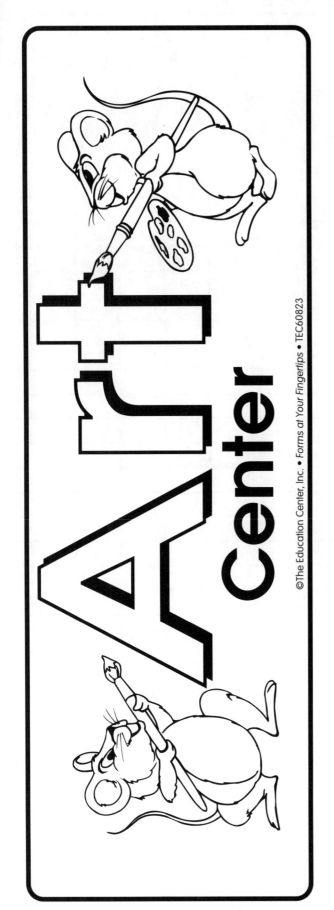

Art
center

Reading
Area

Math Center

©The Education Center, Inc. • Forms at Your Fingertips • TEC60823

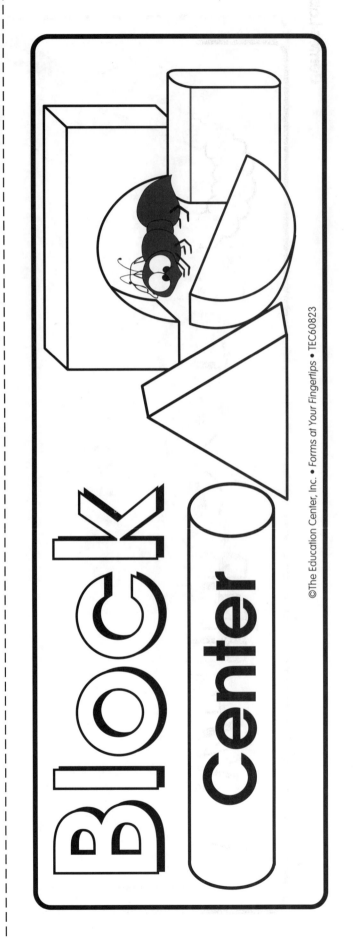

Block Center

©The Education Center, Inc. • Forms at Your Fingertips • TEC60823

Writing Center

Dramatic-Play Area

Classroom Helpers List

Classroom Helpers	Line Leader	Door Holder	Messenger	Snack Helper	Calendar Helper	Pet Helper	Plant Helper		
1.									
2.									
3.									
4.									
5.									
6.									
7.									
8.									
9.									
10.									
11.									
12.									
13.									
14.									
15.									
16.									
17.									
18.									
19.									
20.									
21.									
22.									
23.									
24.									
25.									
26.									
27.									
28.									
29.									
30.									

Classroom Rules Poster

Classroom Rules

Note to the teacher: Program this page with your classroom rules. Then make a class supply to send one home with each student. Make one enlarged copy of this page, color it, and then display it in your classroom.

Playground Rules

Note to the teacher: Program this page with your school playground rules. Then make a class supply to send one home with each student. Make one enlarged copy of this page, color it, and then display it in your classroom.

Homework Policy

Supplies to keep at home:

Note to the teacher: Program this page with your classroom homework policy. Then make a class supply to send one home with each student. Make one enlarged copy of this page, color it, and then display it in your classroom.

Rewards

Behavior Policy

Note to the Teacher: Program this page with your classroom behavior policy. Then make a class supply to send one home with each student. Make one enlarged copy of this page, color it, and then display it in your classroom.

Behavior Documentation

Grade: _____ Room No.: _____

Teacher: _____

Dates: _____

Student Name	Behavior	Date	Action Taken	Parent Contact/Response

Award Coupons and Tokens

Good Work Coupon
Redeem this coupon for
_____
_____
_____
_____
(student name)
©The Education Center, Inc. • *Forms at Your Fingertips* • TEC60823

Good Work Coupon
Redeem this coupon for
_____
_____
_____
_____
(student name)
©The Education Center, Inc. • *Forms at Your Fingertips* • TEC60823

Good Work Coupon
Redeem this coupon for
_____
_____
_____
_____
(student name)
©The Education Center, Inc. • *Forms at Your Fingertips* • TEC60823

Good Work Coupon
Redeem this coupon for
_____
_____
_____
_____
(student name)
©The Education Center, Inc. • *Forms at Your Fingertips* • TEC60823

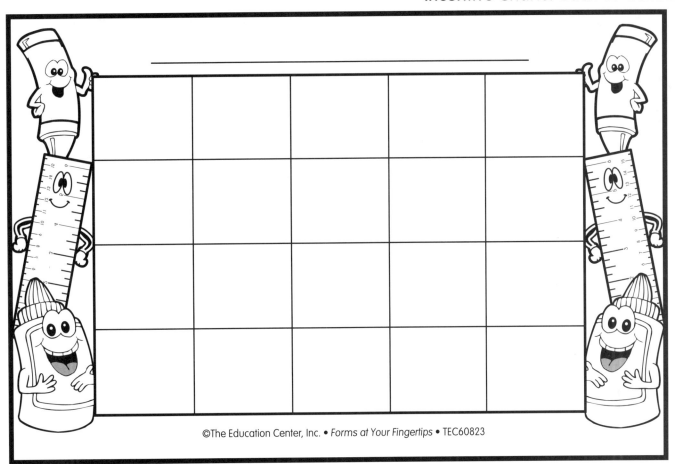

©The Education Center, Inc. • *Forms at Your Fingertips* • TEC60823

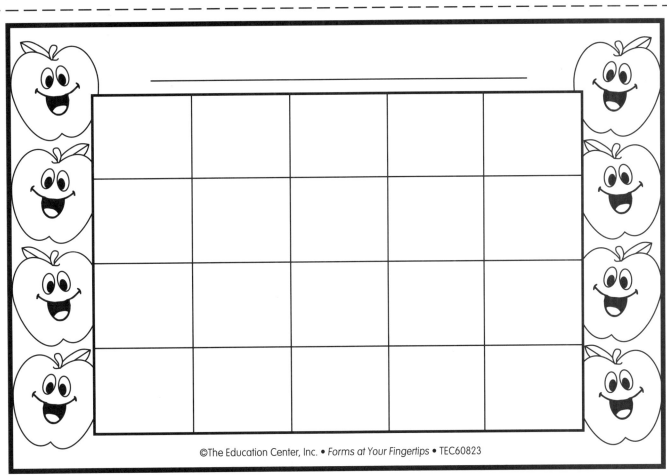

©The Education Center, Inc. • *Forms at Your Fingertips* • TEC60823

Incentive Charts: Fall

©The Education Center, Inc. • *Forms at Your Fingertips* • TEC60823

©The Education Center, Inc. • *Forms at Your Fingertips* • TEC60823

©The Education Center, Inc. • *Forms at Your Fingertips* • TEC60823

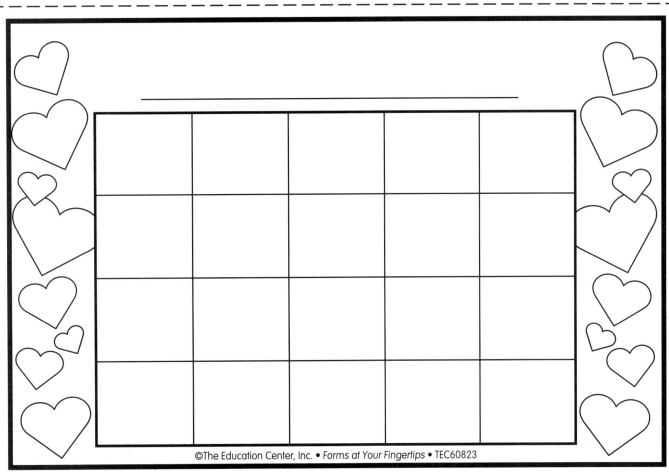

©The Education Center, Inc. • *Forms at Your Fingertips* • TEC60823

Incentive Charts: Spring

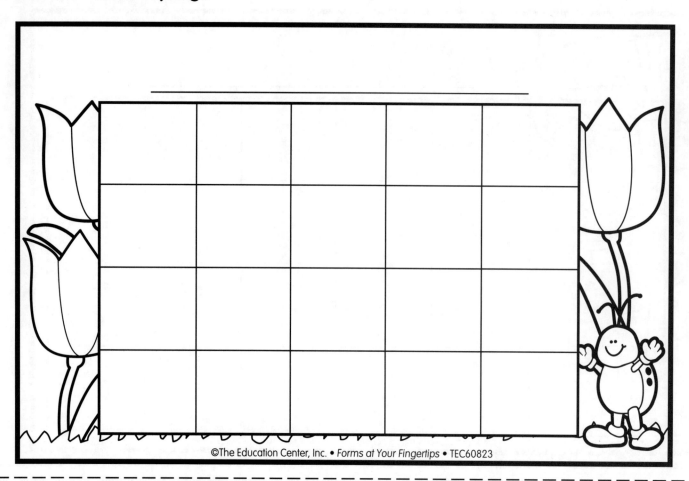

©The Education Center, Inc. • *Forms at Your Fingertips* • TEC60823

©The Education Center, Inc. • *Forms at Your Fingertips* • TEC60823

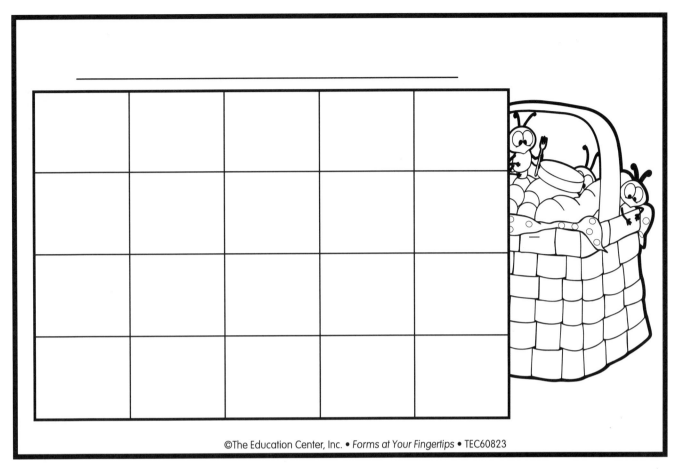

All About _____
name

This is me.

This is my family.

This is how I feel about

—school.

—reading.

—watching TV.

—playing with friends.

—learning new things.

—me.

The things I like are _____

_____

The things I do not like are _____

_____

I am good at _____

_____

I wish I could _____

_____

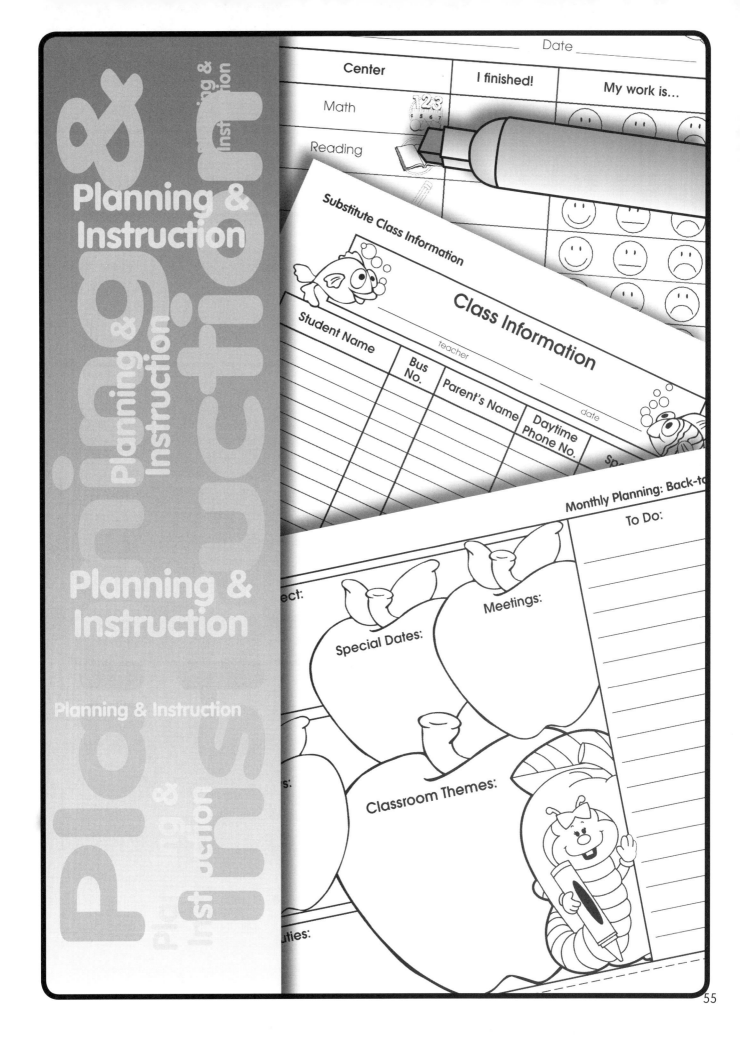

Planning & Instruction

YEARLY PLANNING CALENDAR

AUGUST	SEPTEMBER	OCTOBER	NOVEMBER	DECEMBER	JANUARY

YEARLY PLANNING CALENDAR

FEBRUARY	MARCH	APRIL	MAY	JUNE	JULY

To Do:

Meetings:

Special Dates:

Materials to Collect:

Classroom Themes:

Birthdays:

Duties:

Note to the teacher: At the beginning of each month, make a copy of this page to use for monthly planning.

To Do:

Meetings:

Materials to Collect:

Special Dates:

FALL

Classroom Themes:

Birthdays:

Duties:

Note to the teacher: At the beginning of each month, make a copy of this page to use for monthly planning.

To Do:

Meetings:

Special Dates:

Materials to Collect:

WINTER
Classroom Themes:

Birthdays:

Duties:

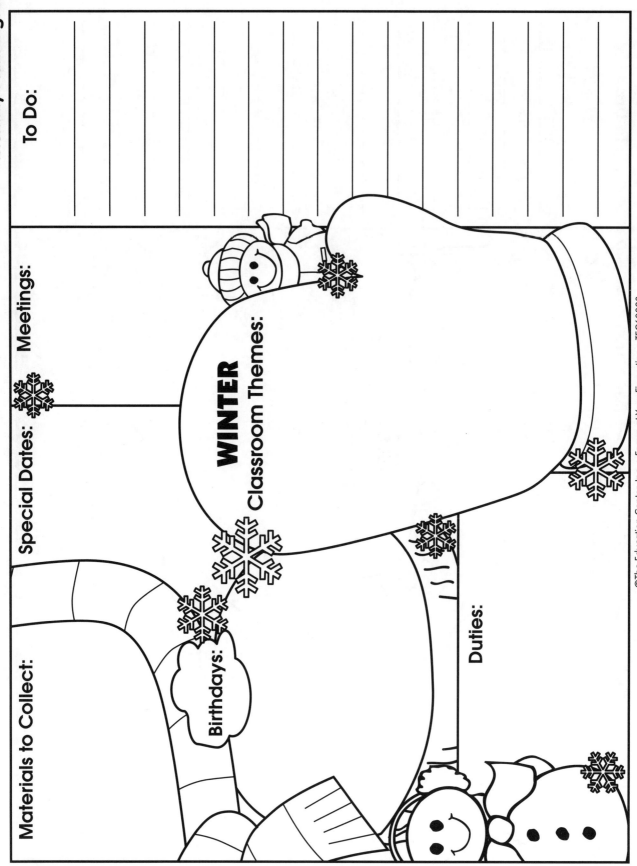

Note to the teacher: At the beginning of each month, make a copy of this page to use for monthly planning.

Monthly Planning: Spring

To Do:

Meetings:

Special Dates:

Materials to Collect:

Spring
Classroom Themes:

Birthdays:

Duties:

Note to the teacher: At the beginning of each month, make a copy of this page to use for monthly planningt

To Do:

Meetings:

Special Dates:

Summer
Classroom Themes:

Materials to Collect:

Birthdays:

Duties:

Note to the teacher: At the beginning of each month, make a copy of this page to use for monthly planning.

Weekly Plan

Monday	Tuesday	Wednesday
Thursday	Friday	Notes

Preschool Plans

We're Learning About _____

Date _____

Circle-Time Fun

Learning Centers

Language:

Math:

Art:

Discovery:

Manipulatives:

Sand/Water:

Blocks:

Dramatic Play:

Movement

Stories to Read

Special Students

Small-Group Activities

Notes

Don't Forget!

M T W T F

date

Top priority:

☐ ☐ ☐ ☐ ☐ ☐ ☐ ☐ ☐

Appointments:

Don't Forget!

M T W T F

date

Top priority:

☐ ☐ ☐ ☐ ☐ ☐ ☐ ☐ ☐

Appointments:

SCHOOL INFORMATION

General Information

Teacher _____

Room Number _____

Principal _____

Assistant Principal _____

Secretary _____

Nurse _____

Guidance Counselor _____

Custodian _____

Grade-Level Teachers _____

Aide(s) _____

Special Teachers (name, day of week, time)

Music _____

Art _____

P.E. _____

Media Specialist _____

Resource _____

Other _____

Children With Special Needs

Health _____

Supervision _____

Learning _____

CLASSROOM PROCEDURES

Start of Day _____

_____

Attendance _____

_____

_____

Fire Drill _____

_____

Recess _____

_____

Lunch/Milk Count _____

_____

Restroom Break _____

_____

Behavior Policy/Discipline _____

_____

Free Time _____

_____

End of Day _____

_____

Student Pull-Outs For Special Programs:

Name	Class	Day/Time

Helpful Students: _____

_____

Substitute Class Information

CLASS INFORMATION

_____   _____
teacher   date

Student Name	Bus No.	Parent's Name	Daytime Phone No.	Special Needs
1.				
2.				
3.				
4.				
5.				
6.				
7.				
8.				
9.				
10.				
11.				
12.				
13.				
14.				
15.				
16.				
17.				
18.				
19.				
20.				
21.				
22.				
23.				
24.				
25.				
26.				
27.				
28.				
29.				
30.				

SUBSTITUTE LESSON PLANS

Time	Monday	Tuesday	Wednesday	Thursday	Friday

Free-Time Activities _____

_____

_____

_____

_____

Welcome to Room

EMERGENCY LESSON PLANS

Subject	Lesson

A NOTE FROM THE SUB

_____   _____
substitute's name   date

What information or items did you need but couldn't find?

_____

_____

_____

What was most helpful to you today?

_____

_____

_____

What, if any, problems did you encounter?

_____

_____

_____

Please list information (positive or negative) about students below.

_____

_____

_____

_____

Thank you for your help!

's

Journal

Name

My Home Reading

Name _____

Monday
Book Title _____

_____

Today I read for _____ minutes! _____
(parent initials)

Tuesday
Book Title _____

_____

Today I read for _____ minutes! _____
(parent initials)

Wednesday
Book Title _____

_____

Today I read for _____ minutes! _____
(parent initials)

Thursday
Book Title _____

_____

Today I read for _____ minutes! _____
(parent initials)

Friday
Book Title _____

_____

Today I read for _____ minutes! _____
(parent initials)

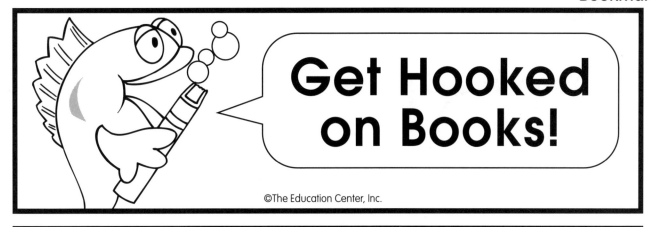

_____
name

is a "Dino-mite" Reader!

Teacher: _____

©The Education Center, Inc. • Forms at Your Fingertips • TEC60823

_____
name

is a "Dino-mite" Reader!

Teacher: _____

©The Education Center, Inc. • Forms at Your Fingertips • TEC60823

Name _____

Work Watcher

How did you do on _____?

Color a face to answer each question.

Did I listen?

Did I do my best?

Am I proud of my work?

Next time I will

Student Evaluation

Name: _____

Work Habits:

☐ Works independently and completes work

☐ Needs some assistance

☐ Needs a great deal of assistance

☐ Is easily distracted

Behavior: _____

Effort/Attitude: _____

Additional comments: _____

Teacher _____

Please sign and return the report to school. Your comments are always appreciated. If you need additional space, use the back of the report or another sheet of paper.

_____
parent's signature

My Centers

Name _____   Date _____

Center		I finished!	My work is…		
Math			☺	😐	☹
Reading			☺	😐	☹
Writing			☺	😐	☹
Language			☺	😐	☹
Manipulatives			☺	😐	☹
Art			☺	😐	☹
Painting			☺	😐	☹
Discovery			☺	😐	☹
Housekeeping			☺	😐	☹
Cooking			☺	😐	☹
			☺	😐	☹
			☺	😐	☹

	Reading	Math	Social Studies	Science	Centers					
1.										
2.										
3.										
4.										
5.										
6.										
7.										
8.										
9.										
10.										
11.										
12.										
13.										
14.										
15.										
16.										
17.										
18.										
19.										
20.										
21.										
22.										
23.										
24.										
25.										
26.										
27.										
28.										
29.										
30.										

Programmable Cards: Back-to-School

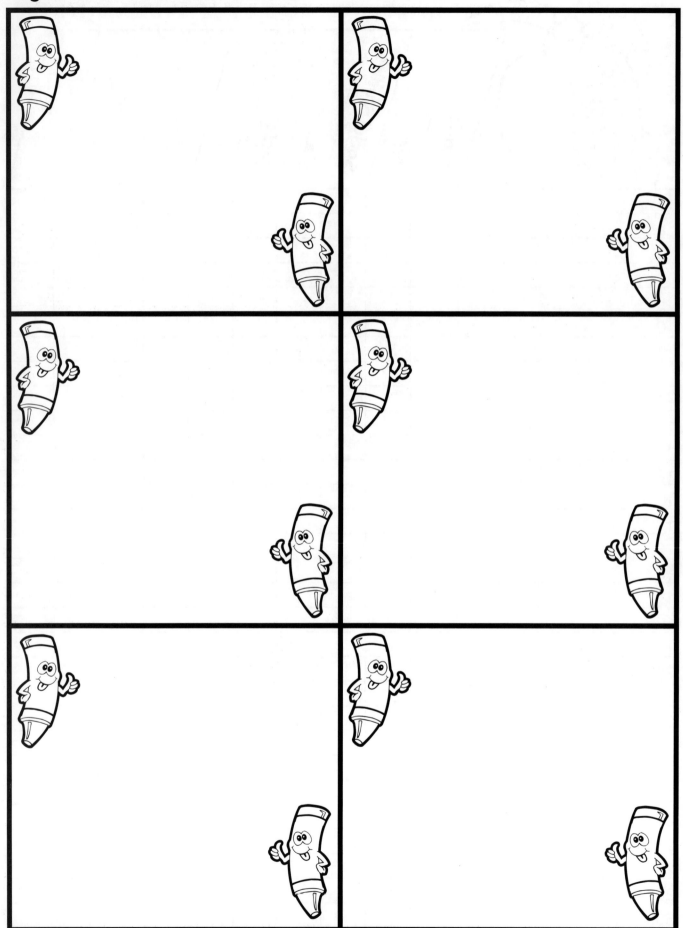

80   ©The Education Center, Inc. • *Forms at Your Fingertips* • TEC60823

Programmable Cards: Winter

Programmable Cards: Summer

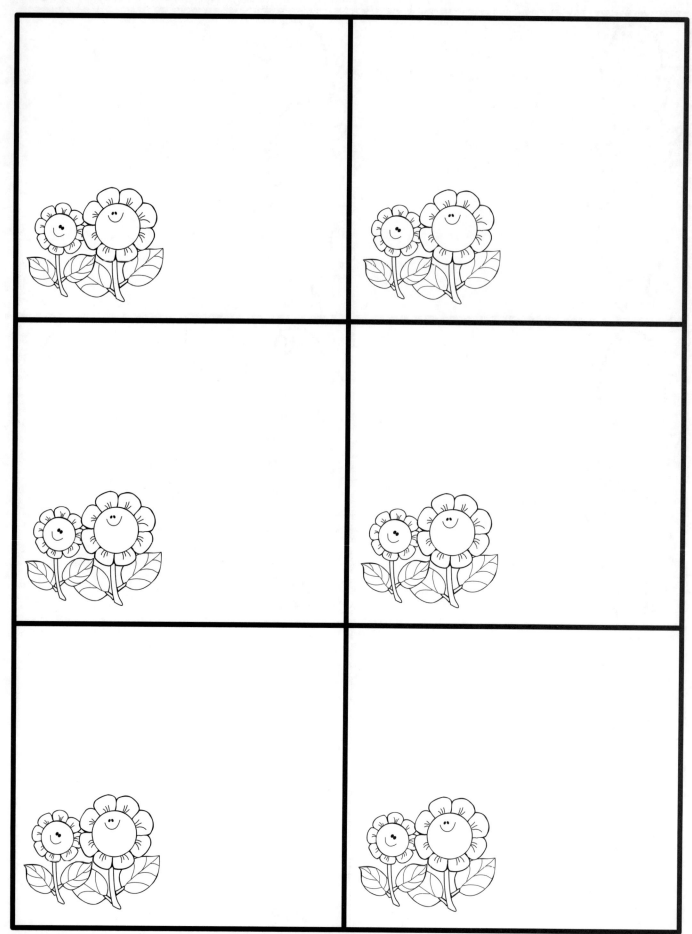

Communications

Communications

Communications

Communications

Communications

Communications

Extra Help Needed

Dear Parent,

_____ needs extra help with

Here are some suggestions for how you can help your ch

Thank you!
Sincerely,

teacher

©The Education Center, Inc. • Forms at Your Fin

Extra Help

Dear Parent,

_____

are some suggestio

Award

_____ is a "beary" good worker!

name

teacher

date

©The Education Center, Inc. • Forms at Your Fingertips • TEC60823

Welcome Letter

Dear _____,

Welcome to _____! I am excited about having you in my class.

Our school day begins at _____. This year we will be
learning about _____
_____
_____
_____

Here are some things you may bring to school:
_____
_____
_____

I am anxious to learn more about you and the things you enjoy.

Your teacher,

_____

_____'s

first day of school was great!

_____ _____
teacher   date

_____'s

first day of school was great!

_____ _____
teacher   date

You're Invited!

Dear Parent,

 You are invited to open house at our school at

_____ on _____,
 _{time}   _{day}

_____.
                        date

We hope to see you there!

Sincerely,

_____
                  teacher

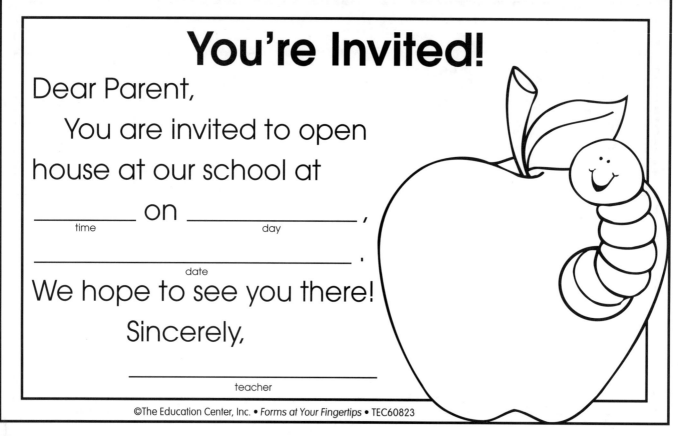

You're Invited!

Dear Parent,

 You are invited to open house at our school at

_____ on _____,
 time   day

_____.
                        date

We hope to see you there!

Sincerely,

_____
                  teacher

Open House

Please sign in.

Parent	Child
1.	
2.	
3.	
4.	
5.	
6.	
7.	
8.	
9.	
10.	
11.	
12.	
13.	
14.	
15.	
16.	
17.	
18.	
19.	
20.	
21.	
22.	
23.	
24.	
25.	
26.	
27.	
28.	
29.	
30.	

I'm glad you're here. Thanks for coming!

Open House Thank-You

Thank you for coming to open house. Your attendance is appreciated! Sincerely,

teacher

©The Education Center, Inc. • *Forms at Your Fingertips* • TEC60823

Thank you for coming to open house. Your attendance is appreciated! Sincerely,

teacher

©The Education Center, Inc. • *Forms at Your Fingertips* • TEC60823

Thank you for coming to open house. Your attendance is appreciated! Sincerely,

teacher

©The Education Center, Inc. • *Forms at Your Fingertips* • TEC60823

Thank you for coming to open house. Your attendance is appreciated! Sincerely,

teacher

©The Education Center, Inc. • *Forms at Your Fingertips* • TEC60823

Dear Parent,
    Your conference for _____
has been scheduled at _____
on _____, _____.

Please complete the bottom portion of this form
    and return it to me as soon as possible.
    I look forward to visiting with you.
        Sincerely,

_____
teacher signature

☐ I plan to attend my child's conference at the scheduled time.
☐ I will need to reschedule our conference. A more convenient time
    for me would be _____.

_____   _____
child's name   parent signature

Dear Parent,
    Your conference for _____
has been scheduled at _____
on _____, _____.

Please complete the bottom portion of this form
    and return it to me as soon as possible.
    I look forward to visiting with you.
        Sincerely,

_____
teacher signature

☐ I plan to attend my child's conference at the scheduled time.
☐ I will need to reschedule our conference. A more convenient time
    for me would be _____.

_____   _____
child's name   parent signature

Parent-Teacher Conference Questionnaire

Dear Parent,

    I am looking forward to meeting with you at our parent-teacher conference. In preparing for our visit, I would like to know more about your child and your areas of concern.

    Please answer the questions below and return the form to me as soon as possible. These insights to your child will help us make the best use of our time together. Thank you for your help!

    Sincerely,

_____
teacher

Cut off and return the bottom portion.

Child's name _____

My child's interests are _____

_____

My child's out-of-school activities include _____

_____

My child learns best by _____

_____

My child's attitude toward school is _____

_____

Topics I am most concerned about include:

___ work habits at school   ___ listening/attention

___ study habits at school   ___ respect for others

___ attitude   ___ skill level in _____

___ self-control   _____

___ relations with friends   ___ other _____

___ self-esteem   ___ other _____

Comments: _____

_____

_____

_____   _____
parent signature   date

Parent-Teacher Conference Report

Student: _____

Persons in Attendance: _____

_____

Date: _____

WORK HABITS

	Excellent	Satisfactory	Needs Improvement	Unsatisfactory
Listens				
Follows directions				
Works independently				
Works accurately				
Works neatly				
Completes work on time				

ATTITUDES

	Excellent	Satisfactory	Needs Improvement	Unsatisfactory
Gets along with others				
Is courteous and cooperates				
Demonstrates self-control				
Shows respect for others				
Cares for personal property				
Assumes responsibility for actions				

Progress and Comments on Academic Areas: _____

_____

_____

_____

_____

_____

_____

_____

_____

_____

_____

Student's Strengths: _____

_____

_____

Areas for Improvement: _____

_____

_____

Actions/Suggestions: _____

_____

_____

Signed: _____   _____
                teacher   parent

Parent/Teacher Conference

Please sign in.

Parent	Child
1.	
2.	
3.	
4.	
5.	
6.	
7.	
8.	
9.	
10.	
11.	
12.	
13.	
14.	
15.	
16.	
17.	
18.	
19.	
20.	
21.	
22.	
23.	
24.	
25.	
26.	
27.	
28.	
30.	

I'm glad you're here. Thanks for coming!

Thank you for coming to parent-teacher conference. Your attendance is appreciated! Sincerely,

teacher

Thank you for coming to parent-teacher conference. Your attendance is appreciated! Sincerely,

teacher

Thank you for coming to parent-teacher conference. Your attendance is appreciated! Sincerely,

teacher

Thank you for coming to parent-teacher conference. Your attendance is appreciated! Sincerely,

teacher

Classroom News

Teacher: _____ Date: _____

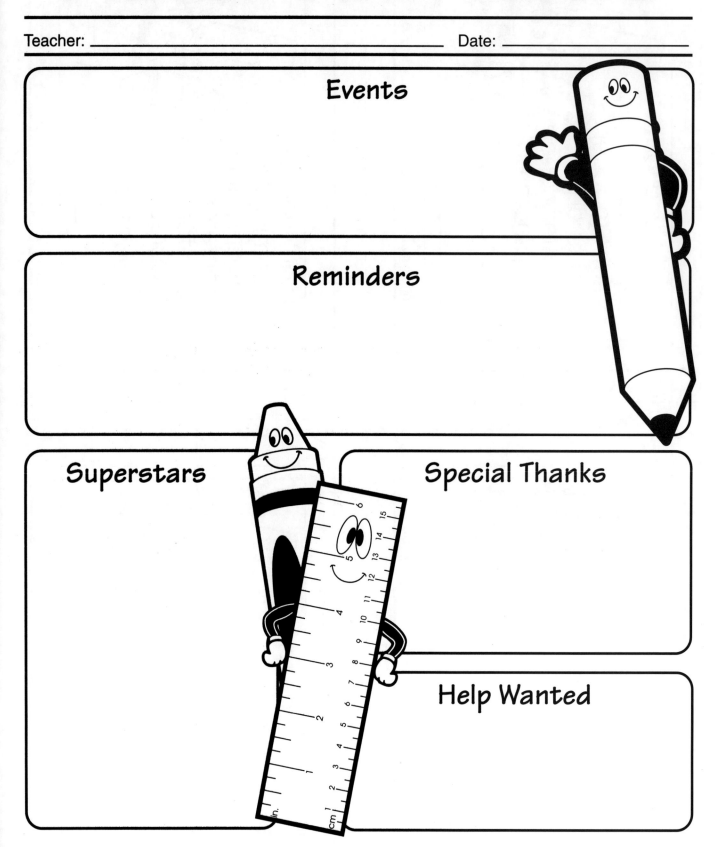

Events

Reminders

Superstars

Special Thanks

Help Wanted

Classroom Times

Teacher: _____ Date: _____

Events

Reminders

Superstars

Special Thanks

Help Wanted

Classroom Times

Teacher: _____ Date: _____

Events

Reminders

Superstars

Special Thanks

Help Wanted

Classroom Times

Teacher: _____ Date: _____

Events

Reminders

Superstars

Special Thanks

Help Wanted

Classroom Times

Teacher: _____   Date: _____

Events

Reminders

Superstars

Special Thanks

Help Wanted

School Note

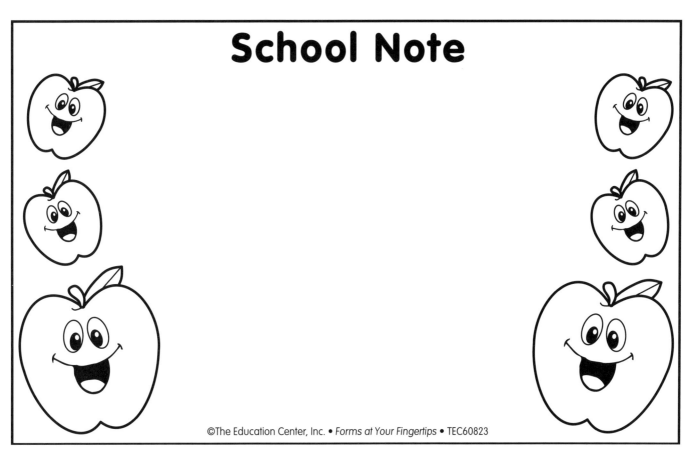

School Note

School Note

School Note

School Note

©The Education Center, Inc. • *Forms at Your Fingertips* • TEC60823

School Note

©The Education Center, Inc. • *Forms at Your Fingertips* • TEC60823

School Note

©The Education Center, Inc. • *Forms at Your Fingertips* • TEC60823

School Note

©The Education Center, Inc. • *Forms at Your Fingertips* • TEC60823

SCHOOL NOTE

 # SCHOOL NOTE

Student Progress Report

Name _____ Date _____

O = Outstanding   S = Satisfactory   N = Needs Practice

Listens Carefully		Treats Others With Respect	
Stays on Task		Follows Class Rules	
Follows Directions		Does His/Her Best Work	

Comments _____

_____

_____

Parent Signature _____

©The Education Center, Inc. • *Forms at Your Fingertips* • TEC60823

- -

Weekly Progress Report

Name _____ Date _____

O = Outstanding   S = Satisfactory   N = Needs Practice

Listens Carefully		Treats Others With Respect	
Stays on Task		Follows Class Rules	
Follows Directions		Does His/Her Best Work	

Comments _____

_____

_____

Parent Signature _____

©The Education Center, Inc. • *Forms at Your Fingertips* • TEC60823

Extra Help Needed

Dear Parent,

_____ needs extra help with _____

_____ .

Here are some suggestions for how you can help your child at home:

_____

_____

_____

Thank you!
Sincerely,

_____   _____
teacher   date

Extra Help Needed

Dear Parent,

_____ needs extra help with _____

_____ .

Here are some suggestions for how you can help your child at home:

_____

_____

_____

Thank you!
Sincerely,

_____   _____
teacher   date

Money Due

Dear Parent,

_____ owes
student

_____ for _____ .
amount   reason

Please return the money to school in this envelope by

_____ .
date

Sincerely,

_____
teacher

Money Due

Dear Parent,

_____ owes
student

_____ for _____ .
amount   reason

Please return the money to school in this envelope by

_____ .
date

Sincerely,

_____
teacher

Money Due

Dear Parent,

_____ owes
student

_____ for _____ .
amount   reason

Please return the money to school in this envelope by

_____ .
date

Sincerely,

_____
teacher

REMINDER!
Library books are due

_____
date

REMINDER!
Library books are due

_____
date

REMINDER!
Library books are due

_____
date

REMINDER!
Library books are due

_____
date

Dear Parent,

   Please remember the following.

Thank you,

_____
teacher

Dear Parent,

_____ 's show-and-tell day is scheduled for _____ _____. Please help your child find something that will fit into his/her book-bag to share with the class. Help your child think of at least one thing to say about the item. Please do not send unsafe or fragile items to school.

Thank you,

_____

Dear Parent,

_____ 's show-and-tell day is scheduled for _____ _____. Please help your child find something that will fit into his/her book-bag to share with the class. Help your child think of at least one thing to say about the item. Please do not send unsafe or fragile items to school.

Thank you,

_____

We're Going on a Field Trip

Dear Parent,

We are planning a trip to _____

_____

on _____ , _____. Your child will

need to bring: • field trip permission form (below)

• _____

• _____

• _____

Keep this note and post it at home as a reminder.

Thank you.

_____
teacher

Cut here and return the form below.

- -

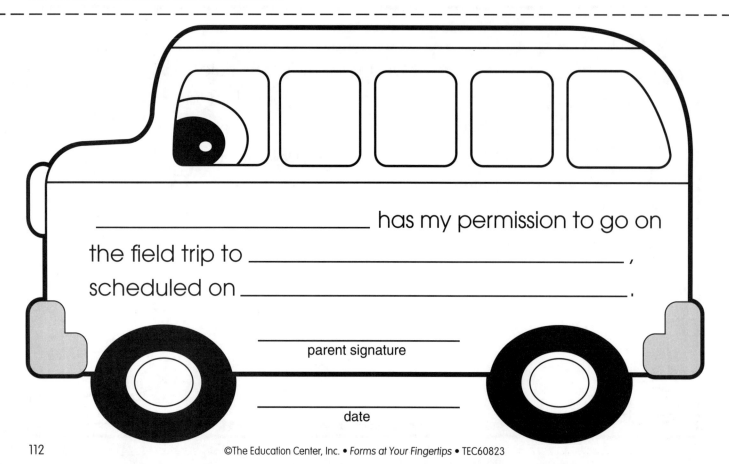

_____ has my permission to go on

the field trip to _____ ,

scheduled on _____ .

_____
parent signature

_____
date

©The Education Center, Inc. • *Forms at Your Fingertips* • TEC60823

Field Trip Volunteer Information

Field Trip Crew

Student's Name	Bus	Parent's Name	Daytime Phone	Special Needs	Schedule

Volunteer _____

School Phone _____

Injury Report

Dear Parent,

This is to report that _____ was

student

injured at school.

Injury: _____

Treatment: _____

Treated by: _____

Follow-up suggestions: _____

_____

Please sign and return this notice. Thank you.

_____ _____

parent signature   teacher signature

Injury Report

Dear Parent,

This is to report that _____ was

student

injured at school.

Injury: _____

Treatment: _____

Treated by: _____

Follow-up suggestions: _____

_____

Please sign and return this notice. Thank you.

_____ _____

parent signature   teacher signature

Parent Volunteer Information

Dear Parent,

It is helpful for me to gather information about my students' parents for upcoming projects and events. I value your interests and expertise, and I encourage you to share talents with us. Please complete the form below and return it to school as soon as possible. Thanks!

Sincerely,

_____
teacher signature

Parent _____ Child _____

Address _____ Phone _____

I enjoy the following hobbies: _____

My profession is _____

I can contribute by
☐ being a parent helper   ☐ making phone calls   ☐ going on field trips
☐ supplying materials   ☐ making projects at home ☐ other _____

Comments: _____
_____

©The Education Center, Inc. • *Forms at Your Fingertips* • TEC60823

Parent Volunteer Information

Dear Parent,

It is helpful for me to gather information about my students' parents for upcoming projects and events. I value your interests and expertise, and I encourage you to share talents with us. Please complete the form below and return it to school as soon as possible. Thanks!

Sincerely,

_____
teacher signature

Parent _____ Child _____

Address _____ Phone _____

I enjoy the following hobbies: _____

My profession is _____

I can contribute by
☐ being a parent helper   ☐ making phone calls   ☐ going on field trips
☐ supplying materials   ☐ making projects at home ☐ other _____

Comments: _____
_____

©The Education Center, Inc. • *Forms at Your Fingertips* • TEC60823

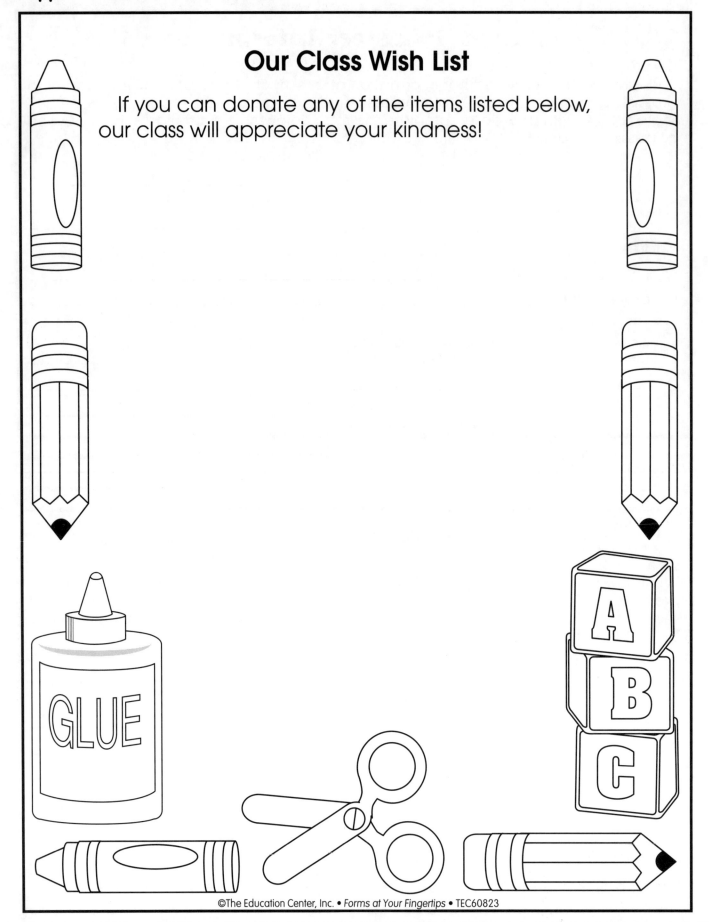

Our Class Wish List

If you can donate any of the items listed below, our class will appreciate your kindness!

GLUE

A
B
C

©The Education Center, Inc. • *Forms at Your Fingertips* • TEC60823

Note to the Teacher: Program this page with your classroom wish list. Then make a class supply and send one copy home with each student. Make one enlarged copy of this page, color it, and then display it in your classroom.

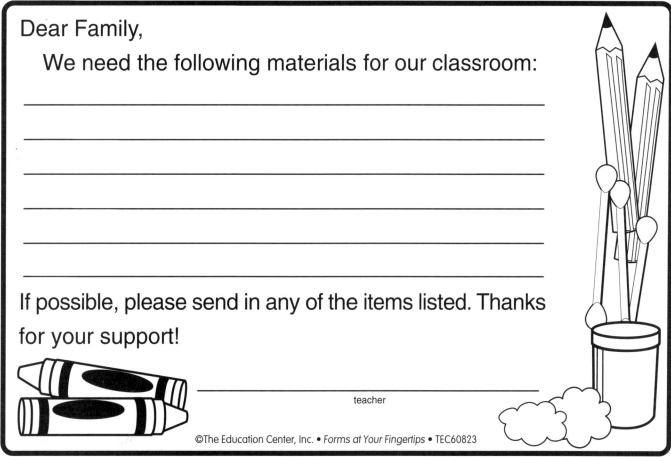

Dear Family,

We need the following materials for our classroom:

_____

_____

_____

_____

_____

_____

If possible, please send in any of the items listed. Thanks for your support!

_____
teacher

©The Education Center, Inc. • *Forms at Your Fingertips* • TEC60823

Dear Family,

We need the following materials for our classroom:

_____

_____

_____

_____

_____

_____

If possible, please send in any of the items listed. Thanks for your support!

_____
teacher

©The Education Center, Inc. • *Forms at Your Fingertips* • TEC60823

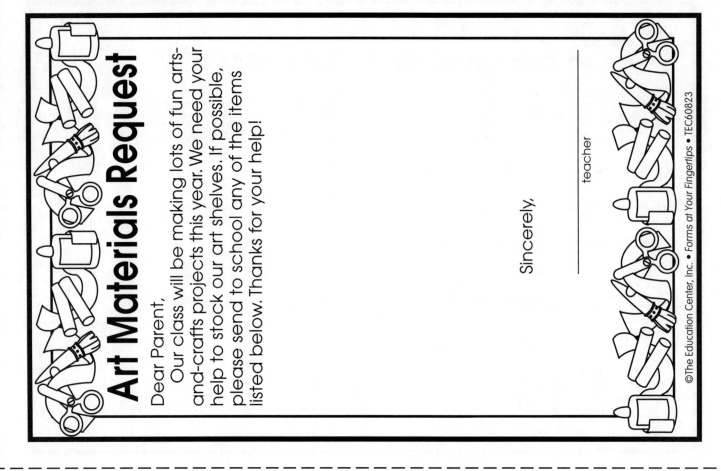

Art Materials Request

Dear Parent,

Our class will be making lots of fun arts-and-crafts projects this year. We need your help to stock our art shelves. If possible, please send to school any of the items listed below. Thanks for your help!

Sincerely,

_____
teacher

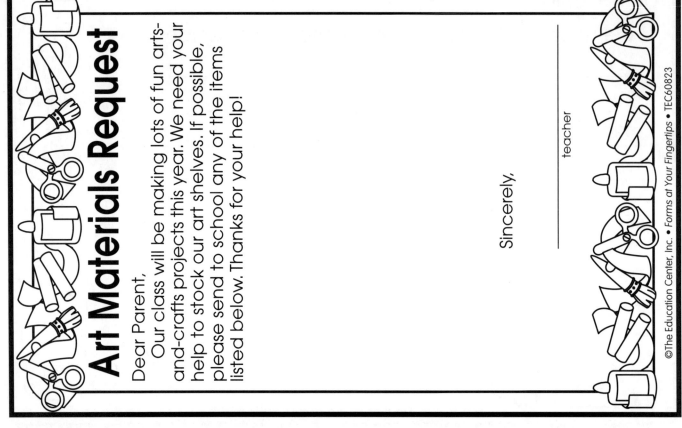

Art Materials Request

Dear Parent,

Our class will be making lots of fun arts-and-crafts projects this year. We need your help to stock our art shelves. If possible, please send to school any of the items listed below. Thanks for your help!

Sincerely,

_____
teacher

Dear Parent or Guardian,
    Our class is preparing for some fun special projects. Please help us out by sending in the following materials:

_____

_____

_____

Thanks for your help!

_____
teacher

Dear Parent or Guardian,
    Our class is preparing for some fun special projects. Please help us out by sending in the following materials:

_____

_____

_____

Thanks for your help!

_____
teacher

Dear Parent,
  With your help, we'll be cooking up something special in our classroom!

What's cooking? _____
name of recipe

What the cooks need:

_____ _____ _____

_____ _____ _____

Please help our budding chefs by supplying the item(s) listed above. We'll need all our ingredients by _____.
date

Let me know if you'll be unable to send in the items requested. Thank you for helping us cook up some learning fun!

Sincerely,

_____
teacher

©The Education Center, Inc. • *Forms at Your Fingertips* • TEC60823

Dear Parent,
  With your help, we'll be cooking up something special in our classroom!

What's cooking? _____
name of recipe

What the cooks need:

_____ _____ _____

_____ _____ _____

Please help our budding chefs by supplying the item(s) listed above. We'll need all our ingredients by _____.
date

Let me know if you'll be unable to send in the items requested. Thank you for helping us cook up some learning fun!

Sincerely,

_____
teacher

©The Education Center, Inc. • *Forms at Your Fingertips* • TEC60823

WE'RE HAVING A SPECIAL PROGRAM

Event: _____

Date: _____

Time: _____

Place: _____

You can help us by _____

_____

_____

Sincerely,

_____
teacher's signature

WE'RE HAVING A SPECIAL PROGRAM

Event: _____

Date: _____

Time: _____

Place: _____

You can help us by _____

_____

_____

Sincerely,

_____
teacher's signature

Dear Parent,

Our Fall party will be at _____
time

on _____ , _____ .
day   date

We will celebrate by _____

_____ .

If you would like to help, please check one of the boxes below and return this note to school. I will contact you with additional information.

☐ I will provide snacks.
☐ I will help in the classroom.
☐ other _____

Sincerely,

_____
teacher signature

_____
parent signature

©The Education Center, Inc. • *Forms at Your Fingertips* • TEC60823

Dear Parent,

Our Fall party will be at _____
time

on _____ , _____
day   date

We will celebrate by _____

_____ .

If you would like to help, please check one of the boxes below and return this note to school. I will contact you with additional information.

☐ I will provide snacks.
☐ I will help in the classroom.
☐ other _____

Sincerely,

_____
teacher signature

_____
parent signature

©The Education Center, Inc. • *Forms at Your Fingertips* • TEC60823

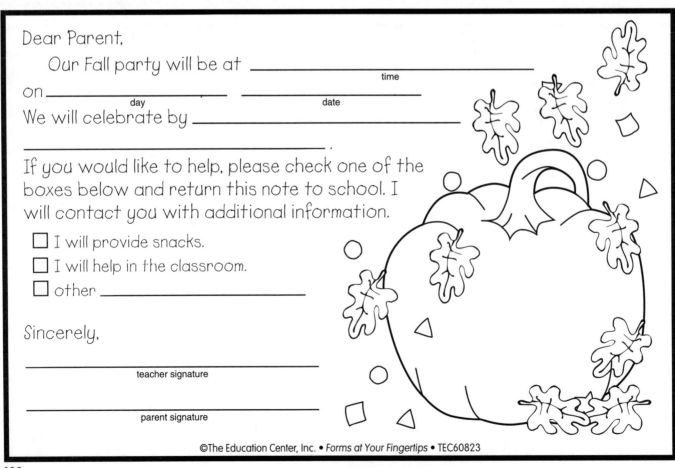

Holiday Party

Dear Parent,

Our holiday party will be at _____

time

on _____ , _____ .

day   date

We will celebrate by _____

_____ .

If you would like to help, please check one of the boxes below and return this note to school.

☐ I will provide food. _____

☐ I will help in the classroom.

☐ other _____

Sincerely,

_____   _____

parent signature   teacher signature

©The Education Center, Inc. • *Forms at Your Fingertips* • TEC60823

Winter Party

Dear Parent,

Our winter party will be at _____

time

on _____ , _____ .

day   date

We will celebrate by _____

_____ .

If you would like to help, please check one of the boxes below and return this note to school.

☐ I will provide food. _____

☐ I will help in the classroom.

☐ other _____

Sincerely,

_____   _____

parent signature   teacher signature

©The Education Center, Inc. • *Forms at Your Fingertips* • TEC60823

Valentine's Day Party

Dear Parent,

Our Valentine's Day party will be at _____
time

on _____, _____ .
day   date

We will celebrate by _____

_____

If you would like to help, please check one of the boxes below and return this note to school.

☐ I will provide food. _____

☐ I will help in the classroom.

☐ other _____

Sincerely,

_____   _____
parent signature   teacher signature

Valentine's Day Party

Dear Parent,

Our Valentine's Day party will be at _____
time

on _____, _____ .
day   date

We will celebrate by _____

_____

If you would like to help, please check one of the boxes below and return this note to school.

☐ I will provide food. _____

☐ I will help in the classroom.

☐ other _____

Sincerely,

_____   _____
parent signature   teacher signature

Our Valentine Class List

Boys

Girls

Teachers:

Spring Party

Dear Parent,

Our spring party will be at _____
time

on _____, _____ .
day   date

We will celebrate by _____

_____ .

If you would like to help, please check one of the boxes below and return this note to school.

☐ I will provide food. _____

☐ I will help in the classroom.

☐ other _____

Sincerely,

_____
teacher signature

_____
parent signature

©The Education Center, Inc. • *Forms at Your Fingertips* • TEC60823

Spring Party

Dear Parent,

Our spring party will be at _____
time

on _____, _____ .
day   date

We will celebrate by _____

_____ .

If you would like to help, please check one of the boxes below and return this note to school.

☐ I will provide food. _____

☐ I will help in the classroom.

☐ other _____

Sincerely,

_____
teacher signature

_____
parent signature

©The Education Center, Inc. • *Forms at Your Fingertips* • TEC60823

End-of-the-Year Party

Dear Parent,

Our end-of-the-year party will be at _____
time

on _____ , _____ .
day   date

We will celebrate by _____

_____ .

If you would like to help, please check one of the boxes below and return this note to school.

☐ I will provide food. _____

☐ I will help in the classroom.

☐ other _____

Sincerely,

_____
teacher signature

_____
parent signature

©The Education Center, Inc. • *Forms at Your Fingertips* • TEC60823

End-of-the-Year Party

Dear Parent,

Our end-of-the-year party will be at _____
time

on _____ , _____ .
day   date

We will celebrate by _____

_____ .

If you would like to help, please check one of the boxes below and return this note to school.

☐ I will provide food. _____

☐ I will help in the classroom.

☐ other _____

Sincerely,

_____
teacher signature

_____
parent signature

©The Education Center, Inc. • *Forms at Your Fingertips* • TEC60823

YOU'RE A TREAT!

name

Happy Halloween!

teacher

HAPPY HOLIDAYS

name

From Your Teacher

name

Happy Valentine's Day From Your Teacher

HAPPY BIRTHDAY!

name

teacher

date

Get Well Soon!

We miss you, _____.

From _____

We are glad you're back!

To: _____

From: _____

_____

name

Thank you for the gift!

From _____

You're Sweet,

_____.

name

Thank-you for the gift!

Thank you!

Dear _____,

parent

Thank you for your help

with the _____.

We really appreciate it!

_____'s

teacher

Preschool Class

Thank you!

Dear _____,

parent

Thank you for your help

with the _____.

We really appreciate it!

_____'s

teacher

Kindergarten Class

THANKS, PARTNER!

_____
name

I really appreciate your help.

Sincerely,

_____

THANKS, PARTNER!

_____
name

I really appreciate your help.

Sincerely,

_____

_____
name

is a "beary" good worker!

_____   _____
teacher   date

©The Education Center, Inc. • *Forms at Your Fingertips* • TEC60823

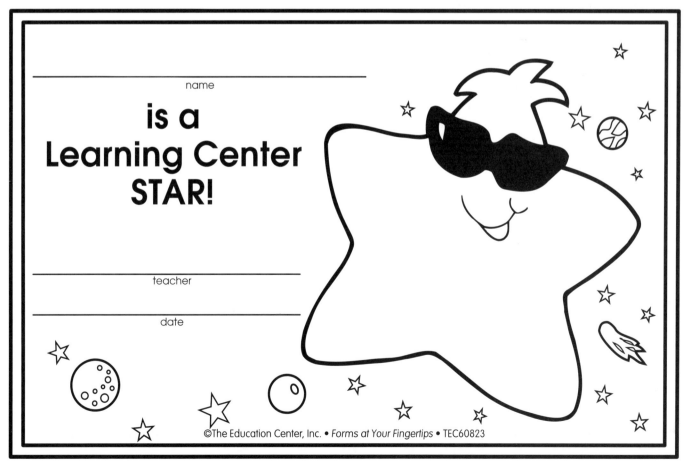

_____
name

is a Learning Center STAR!

_____
teacher

_____
date

©The Education Center, Inc. • *Forms at Your Fingertips* • TEC60823

_____
name

had a "fin-tastic" day!

_____
teacher

_____
date

_____
name

WAS SPOTTED

_____

_____

WAY TO GO!

_____
teacher

_____
date

I'm proud as a pumpkin about

_____
name

_____
teacher

_____
date

©The Education Center, Inc. • _Forms at Your Fingertips_ • TEC60823

_____
name

does gobbling great work!

_____
teacher

_____
date

©The Education Center, Inc. • _Forms at Your Fingertips_ • TEC60823

Award: Winter

Good news bears
reporting!

_____
name

had a great day!

©The Education Center, Inc. • *Forms at Your Fingertips* • TEC60823

"Snow"
Doubt About It!

_____
name

is doing great work!

_____
teacher

_____
date

©The Education Center, Inc. • *Forms at Your Fingertips* • TEC60823

_____
name

has made a
big SPLASH in

_____!

Congratulations!
I'm proud as
a mother duck.

_____
teacher

_____
date

"Some-bunny" has learned how to

_____!

_____
teacher

_____
date

I'm going buggy over

_____ !

Here's why: _____

_____

_____

_____
teacher

_____
date

_____ 's
name
work is in full bloom!
Good job.

_____
teacher

_____
date

_____
name

had a "sea-sational" year in preschool!

_____   _____
teacher   date

_____
name

had a "sea-sational" year in preschool!

_____   _____
teacher   date

Buzzing by to Say...

_____
name

had a great year in Kindergarten!

_____
teacher

_____
date

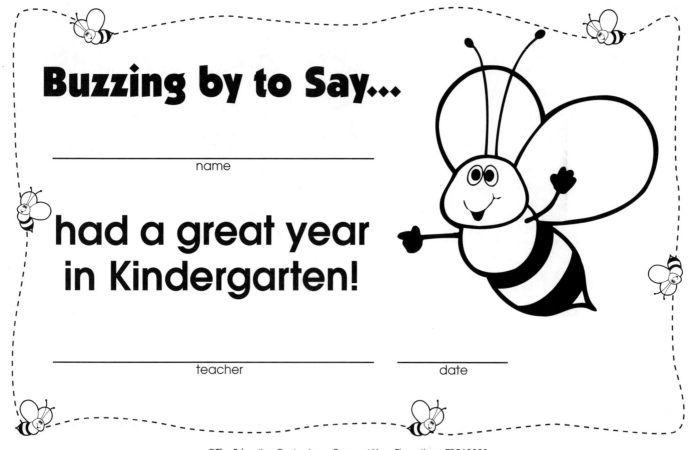

Buzzing by to Say...

_____
name

had a great year in Kindergarten!

_____
teacher

_____
date

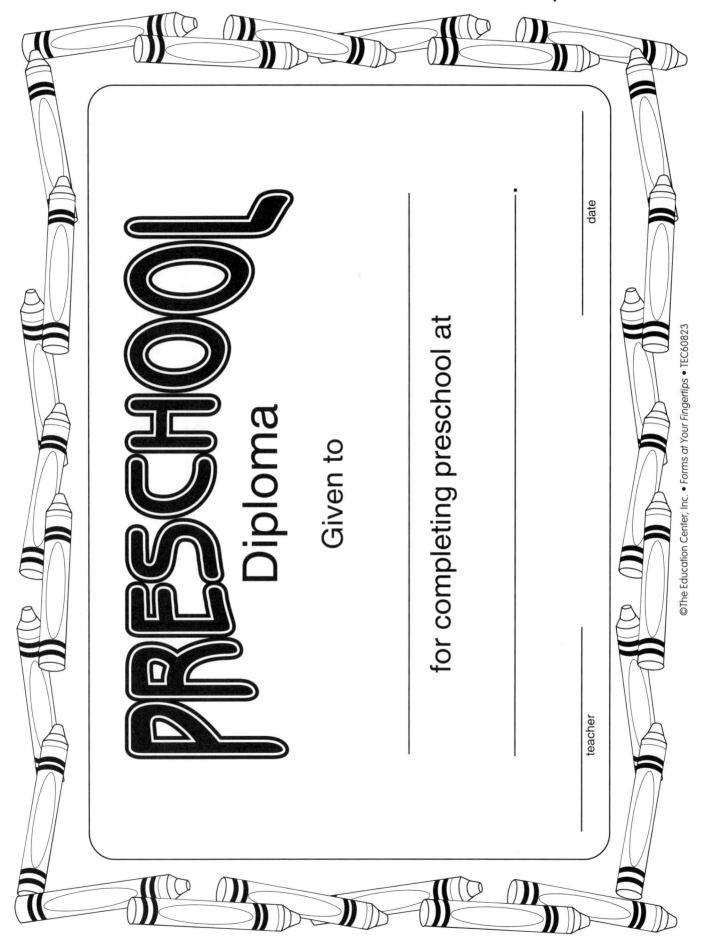

PRESCHOOL

Diploma

Given to

_____

for completing preschool at

_____

_____ .
date

_____
teacher

KINDERGARTEN

Diploma

Given to

for completing kindergarten at

date

teacher